Pebble® Plus

Exploring the Galaxy

The Moon

by Thomas K. Adamson

Consulting Editor: Gail Saunders-Smith, PhD

Consultant: Roger D. Launius, PhD
Chair, Division of Space History
National Air and Space Museum
Smithsonian Institution, Washington, D.C.

Capstone press®

Mankato, Minnesota

Pebble Plus is published by Capstone Press,
151 Good Counsel Drive, P.O. Box 669, Mankato, Minnesota 56002.
www.capstonepub.com

Library of Congress Cataloging-in-Publication Data
Adamson, Thomas K., 1970–
    The Moon / by Thomas K. Adamson.
    p. cm.—(Pebble plus. Exploring the galaxy)
    Includes bibliographical references and index.
    ISBN 978-0-7368-6745-0 (hardcover)
    ISBN 978-1-4296-6289-5 (softcover)
    1. Moon—Juvenile literature. I. Title. II. Series.
QB582.A33 2007
523.3—dc22
                                                         2006023552

Summary: Simple text and photographs describe Earth's moon.

Editorial Credits
Katy Kudela, editor; Kia Adams, set designer; Mary Bode, book designer and illustrator; Jo Miller, photo researcher/photo editor

Photo Credits
Astronomical Society of the Pacific, 19
Getty Images Inc./The Image Bank/Theo Allofs, 7; Stone/Ron Dahlquist, 10–11
Grant Heilman Photography/Chad Ehlers, 4–5
NASA, 21
Photodisc, 9 (both), 13 (both)
Photo Researchers, Inc./NASA, 15, 17
Shutterstock/Carolina K. Smith, M.D., 1; David Woods, cover

Note to Parents and Teachers

The Exploring the Galaxy set supports national science standards related to earth science. This book describes and illustrates the Moon. The photographs support early readers in understanding the text. The repetition of words and phrases helps early readers learn new words. This book also introduces early readers to subject-specific vocabulary words, which are defined in the Glossary section. Early readers may need assistance to read some words and to use the Table of Contents, Glossary, Read More, Internet Sites, and Index sections of the book.

Printed in China
5888/5889/5890   082010

Table of Contents

The Moon

The Moon is the brightest object in the night sky. It reflects the Sun's light.

The Moon seems to change

shape during the month.

The Moon can look round

like a circle.

It can look narrow

like a banana.

The Moon and Earth

The Moon is Earth's satellite.

It moves around Earth

once each month.

The same side of the Moon

always faces Earth.

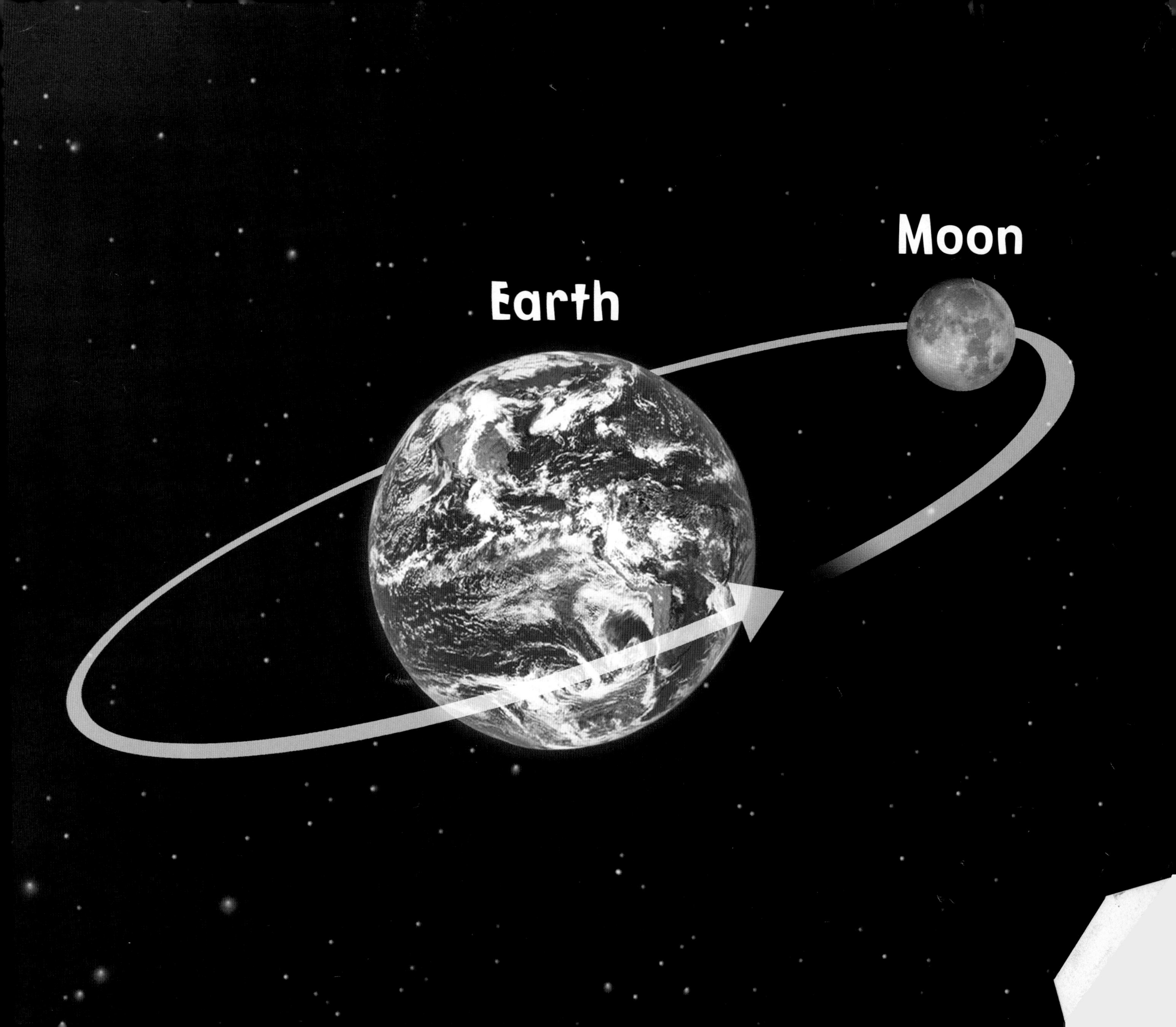
Moon
Earth

The Moon shines
brightly at night.
It looks lighter
in the day.

The Moon is much smaller
than Earth.
If Earth were a tennis ball,
the Moon would be
the size of a marble.

Earth

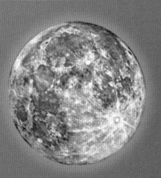

Moon

The Moon's Surface

Gray dust and rocks
cover the Moon.
The Moon's surface
is rough.

16

Craters make

the Moon's surface bumpy.

These holes formed

when objects hit the Moon.

The Moon is not like Earth.

The Moon has no

air or water.

The sky is always black.

Exploring the Moon

Astronauts have landed on

the Moon six times.

They gathered rocks

and soil to study.

Glossary

astronaut—a person who travels into space

crater—a hole made when objects crash into a planet's or moon's surface

Earth—the planet we live on

reflect—to return light from an object; the Moon reflects light from the Sun.

satellite—an object that travels around another object in space; the Moon is Earth's satellite.

Sun—the star that Earth and the other planets move around; the Sun provides light and heat for the planets.

surface—the outside or outermost area of something

Read More

Bredeson, Carmen. *The Moon.* Rookie Read-About Science. New York: Children's Press, 2003.

Olson, Gillia. *Phases of the Moon.* Patterns in Nature. Mankato, Minn.: Capstone Press, 2007.

Winrich, Ralph. *The Moon.* The Solar System. Mankato, Minn.: Capstone Press, 2005.

Internet Sites

FactHound offers a safe, fun way to find Internet sites related to this book. All of the sites on FactHound have been researched by our staff.

Here's how:

1. Visit *www.facthound.com*

2. Choose your grade level.

3. Type in the book ID **0736867457** for age-appropriate sites. You may also browse subjects by clicking on letters, or by clicking on pictures and words.

4. Click on the **Fetch It** button.

FactHound will fetch the best sites for you!

Index

Word Count: 153
Grade: 1
Early-Intervention Level: 15